This book belongs to:

Consultant: Professor Gillian R. Foulger

Published by Ladybird Books Ltd
A Penguin Company
Penguin Books Ltd, 80 Strand, London WC2R 0RL, UK
Penguin Books Australia Ltd, Camberwell, Victoria, Australia
Penguin Books (NZ) Ltd, 67 Apollo Drive, Rosedale, North Shore 0632, New Zealand

1 3 5 7 9 10 8 6 4 2

© LADYBIRD BOOKS MMVII

ISBN: 978-1-84646-524-6

Printed in Italy

Volcanoes

written by Lorraine Horsley
illustrated by Jussi Brightmore

The Earth is made
of a round ball
with layers
over the
top.

crust

The round ball
is called the core.

The middle layer is called the mantle.

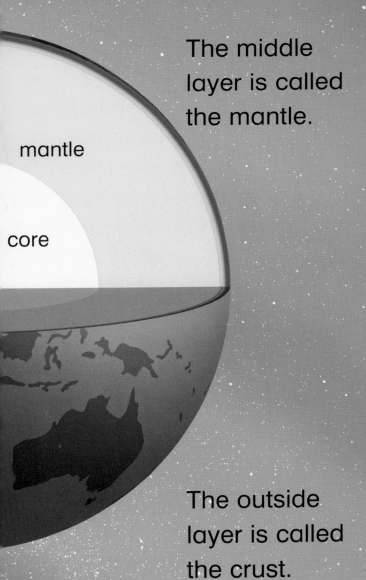

mantle

core

The outside layer is called the crust.

The crust of the Earth is
made of rock.

crust

The crust is the layer of the Earth that we live on.

The crust of the Earth is
made of many pieces.
These pieces are
called plates.

The plates of the Earth are
always moving.

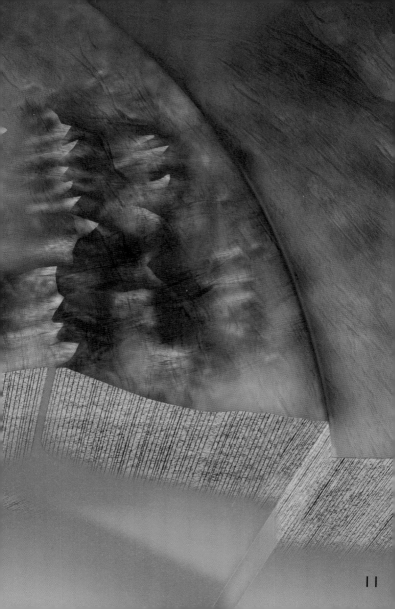

Where the plates meet, magma from the mantle can push up. This is where a volcano erupts.

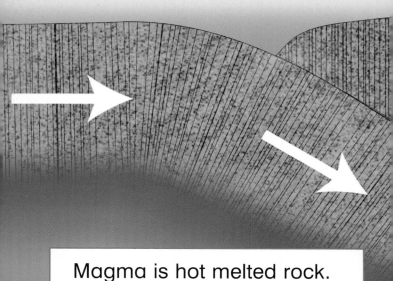

Magma is hot melted rock.

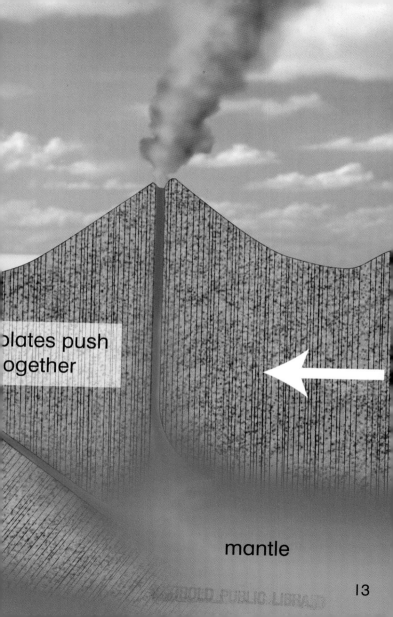

plates push
together

mantle

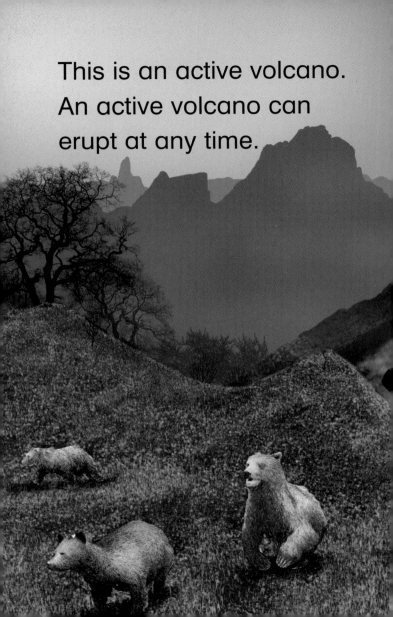

This is an active volcano.
An active volcano can
erupt at any time.

There are about 800 active volcanoes in the world.

Inside the volcano is a chamb
Inside the chamber is hot
magma.

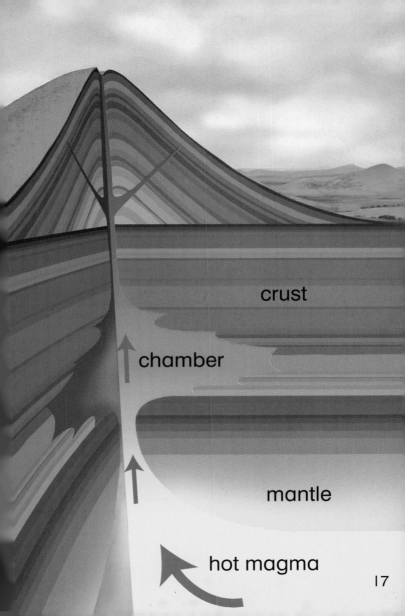

crust

chamber

mantle

hot magma

When the volcano erupts,
hot magma comes out
of the vent.

lava

18

vent

Magma that comes out of the
vent is called lava.

When lava cools down it turns into rock.

Over time, the soil made from volcanic rock becomes good for growing crops.

Sometimes volcanoes
are under the sea.
When they erupt, they
can make islands.

The island of Hawaii was made when a volcano erupted under the sea.

Sometimes volcanoes under the sea can make giant waves. The waves are called tsunamis.

Tsunamis can move 800 kilometres in an hour.

At some volcanoes there are hot springs and mud pools.

Some hot springs can erupt like a fizzy drink. These are called geysers.

Can you remember how a volcano erupts?

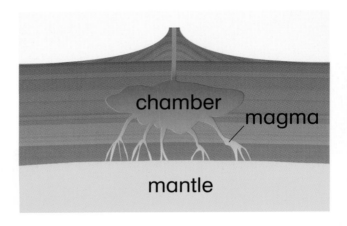

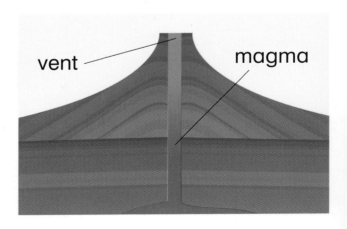

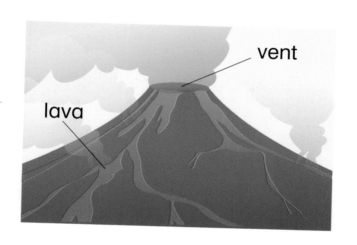

vent

lava

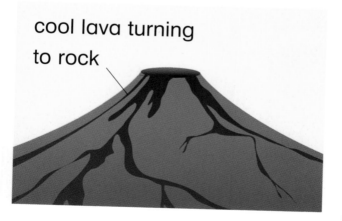

cool lava turning
to rock

Index